ANNETTE HINKLE
FOREWORD BY JAY McINERNEY

SAG HARBOR

100 YEARS OF FILM IN THE VILLAGE

EAST END PRESS
BRIDGEHAMPTON, NEW YORK

SAG HARBOR: 100 YEARS OF FILM IN THE VILLAGE

Copyright © 2017 by Annette Hinkle

All rights reserved. Except for brief passages quoted in newspaper, magazine, radio, television, or online reviews, no portion of this book may be reproduced, distributed, or transmitted in any form or by any means, electronic or mechanical, including photocopying, recording, or information storage or retrieval system, without the prior written permission of the publisher.

Published by
EAST END PRESS
Bridgehampton, NY

ISBN: 978-0-9975304-3-8

FIRST EDITION

Book Design by Neuwirth & Associates, Inc.

Manufactured in Canada

10 9 8 7 6 5 4 3 2 1

For my husband, Adam, who shares my taste in film, and my daughter Sophie, who does not, yet bravely endured more than one screening at the Sag Harbor Cinema.

Also, for the people of Sag Harbor for whom going to the movies has long been a defining feature of a life well-lived in this small village.

Annette Hinkle

SAG HARBOR
100 YEARS OF FILM IN THE VILLAGE

CONTENTS

Foreword by Jay McInerney 9

Introduction 13

PART ONE: THE EARLY DAYS • 1907–1935 25

PART TWO: FROM SILENT TO CINEMASCOPE • 1936–1978 57

PART THREE: STANDING THE TEST OF TIME • 1978–2016 95

A Word From The Sag Harbor Partnership 125

Selected Bibliography 126

Acknowledgments 128

PHOTO COURTESY OF JAKE RAJAS

For as long as any of us could remember, the big red letters floating above main street on the white façade of the cinema situated us and grounded us, reminding us, if perhaps we'd had one too many at the bar in the American Hotel, across the street, of just where we were: SAG HARBOR. The neon sign had been serving this function since the thirties. There were older structures on Main Street, but the art deco façade was the town's signature landmark, beloved even of those who'd never been inside the historic theater. On the morning of December 17, I joined a knot of somber spectators staring at the gap between two scorched, smoldering storefronts; the night before the façade—with its iconic sign—had been demolished after suffering irreparable damage in a pre-dawn conflagration. The storefronts on either side were charred while the branches of the trees nearby glistened, encased with silvery ice in the aftermath of the fire hoses.

Fire has been a constant in the history of the town, ravaging and reshaping the landscape of Main Street again and again since the town's incorporation in 1727. But this was the first major blaze of recent memory, and indeed the idea that a landmark could go up in smoke seemed almost anachronistic—which only added to the sense of shock. Like many local residents I'd spent many hours inside the theater; gaping at the carnage that morning, I assumed the theater was destroyed, but happily, the interior, beyond the lobby, was intact, except for some smoke and water damage.

OPPOSITE: PHOTO COURTESY OF TULLA BOOTH

The first theater built on the site, George's Theatre, built by one George Kiernan, opened its doors in the fall of 1915. In 1927 the building was purchased by Michael Glynne—who owned other motion picture palaces in the East End of Long Island—and was renamed Glynne's Sag Harbor Theatre. Two years later the theater screened *Kitty*, believed to be the first talking picture shown on the East End.

The theater familiar to most of us came into being in the mid-thirties when the facility received an extensive renovation under the supervision of John Eberson, a renowned designer of theaters. The original structure was demolished, replaced by a new steel and concrete auditorium with 600 seats as well as a new lobby, box office, and façade, decorated with the famous blue and red neon Sag Harbor sign. The new cinema's debut feature was Shirley Temple's *Captain January*.

Film buff Gerald Mallow purchased the theater in 1978, initiating minor interior renovations. Mallow's biggest innovation was in programming; he was a foreign cinema buff and, beginning with the French film *Madame Rosa*, has brought hundreds of foreign films to the East End, along with more mainstream domestic fare. The cinema has also hosted many local premieres that tended to be studded with the more illustrious residents of the area, which has always been a magnet for artists and writers.

I've spent many happy hours here in the dark, greeting friends and neighbors as we find our seats, and later, often lingering in the popcorn-scented lobby or the sidewalk outside the theater on a sultry summer night, or a chilly winter afternoon, to discuss what we'd just seen. With the help of some of these same friends and neighbors, I look forward to a new incarnation of this essential Sag Harbor institution.

JAY MCINERNEY
July 2017

On the morning of December 16, 2016, Sag Harbor's Main Street changed drastically over the course of a few hours. It started with a spark, a small flame at the rear of a collection of buildings. Fanned by strong winds, it quickly grew into a massive blaze and despite the efforts of hundreds of volunteer firefighters from across the region battling the flames in frigid temperatures, several buildings were ultimately destroyed.

Among them was the iconic Sag Harbor Cinema.

To those who didn't have a personal relationship with the place, it's difficult to understand how much it meant to those who did. After all, it was just a building—a simple movie theater with an unassuming white stucco façade and the words "SAG HARBOR" spelled out in a basic art deco font, neon tubes running through red letters punctuated by an underscoring of blue.

Red, white, blue. Those patriotic colors and those simple letters were the defining markers of this truly quintessential American village—probably as true as any that can still be found in rare corners of the country where Main Street hasn't been abandoned in favor of cul-de-sacs, strip malls, and an overabundance of traffic lights.

For 80 years, the Sag Harbor Cinema defined this village. Built in 1936, between two World Wars and in the midst of the Great Depression, it was plainspoken, free of pretense or outward adornment, yet beautifully elegant in its own way. To a populace struggling to survive in this factory town in

The iconic theater sign
COURTESY OF JAKE RAJAS

those bleak years, the cinema's glowing neon letters must have served as a beacon of hope, both physically and metaphorically. A bright spot in a village that was badly in need of relief—and inside, Sag Harbor's working-class populace found a place that offered refuge, allowing them to escape reality, even if only for a couple hours at a time.

The Sag Harbor Theatre was actually the fourth movie theater to occupy the site. While the outside of the building was a study in understated deco simplicity, the inside offered absolute fantasy. Elegant in its early years, it aged gracefully, marking the passage of time by seeming to defy it so completely.

The beautiful thing about the theater was that for the eight decades it stood, it remained the same. As the world beyond transformed, grew, suffered, went to war and became jaded, within those four walls life appeared to remain a perpetual constant.

In the 1970s and early 1980s, when the grand movie palaces around the country were carved up into multiplexes so several movies could be shown at once, the Sag Harbor Cinema remained a quirky anachronism—a single-screen venue showing one film at a time. And in its final four decades, under the ownership of Gerald Mallow who bought the place in 1978, those offerings catered primarily to the tastes of lovers of independent films, foreign features, and documentaries.

During those years at the Sag Harbor Cinema, the movies focused on artistry, not the bottom line. In an era driven by high corporate returns, that may have been the most endearing feature of the place in its final years. Here, there were no commercials, coming attractions, corporate logos or pleas to visit the concession stand. The films simply began rolling at the predetermined time whether you were in your seat or not, and even on the busiest summer weekends you'd likely find only a couple dozen people in attendance. In the off-season when shows ran Thursday through Sunday, it was entirely possible you could have the place all to yourself.

"At the Movies" oil painting by Lewis Zacks
COURTESY OF FRAN CASTAN

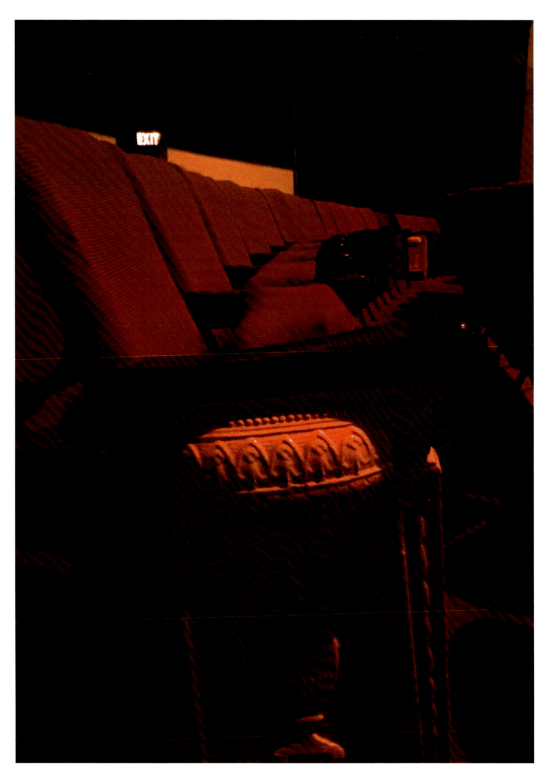

Interior of the Sag Harbor Cinema
COURTESY OF GAIL GALLAGHER

And over the course of its life, it was magical—a place for big dreams, first dates, and stolen kisses—an old-fashioned cinema that was totally unaware of its own charmingly shabby authenticity.

Even in recent years, it was easy to imagine the sense of wonder that greeted theater-goers the first time they walked through the doors, because it was all still there. The mirrored entrance led to the cash window where tickets were purchased. Red carpeting, velvet ropes, and chandeliers ushered guests past the candy counter and the quintessential ladies room, which boasted a pink sink and a lounge furnished with a round mirror and faded settee. Vintage deco signage marked the exits, and once your ticket was torn (often by the same person who sold the tickets and ran the concession stand), a gently sloping corridor took you downward, subtly urging you past the red velvet curtains and into the dimly lit cinema where you'd find your seat and wait for the show to begin.

As time went on, the Sag Harbor Cinema remained an incongruous throwback with the letters on its façade announcing in no uncertain terms not only where you were, but also where this village has been. And for 80 years, at its heart the cinema stood sentinel over a Main Street and a community, which time and time again was forced to reinvent itself.

Geographically speaking, Sag Harbor may be situated in the part of eastern Long Island known as The Hamptons, those beachside resorts with a reputation for excess and privilege, but this comparatively modest village has always gone its own way and has never felt much affinity for its affluent neighbors to the south—and proudly so. That's because Sag Harbor's history lies not in its origins as a resort community for the upper class, but as a working-class town with a blue-collar streak.

While the trades that built the village are long gone, culturally, much of Sag Harbor's population clings stubbornly and proudly to those hard-working roots and values. Ultimately, that's the reason Sag Harbor is, and

Interior of the Sag Harbor Cinema
COURTESY OF MICHAEL HELLER

Interior of the Sag Harbor Cinema
COURTESY OF MICHAEL HELLER

has always been, distinctly unique from its tony neighbors to the south—by virtue of both name and design.

That's also largely what drew writers to Sag Harbor beginning in the mid-twentieth century. They saw the village not as a place to be seen, but as a place to quietly go about their business and do their work. Nelson Algren, Betty Friedan, Thomas Harris and Spalding Gray are just a few of the names associated with Sag Harbor, along with E. L. Doctorow who, in 1983, hosted an advance screening of the Sidney Lumet film *Daniel* at the Sag Harbor Cinema. The film was based on Doctorow's 1971 historical novel *The Book of Daniel*.

Other residents have included playwrights Joe Pintauro, Lanford Wilson, and Jon Robin Baitz, and author Colson Whitehead whose novel *Sag Harbor* is loosely based on his childhood as a summer kid in Eastville. In 2017 Whitehead won the Pulitzer Prize for Fiction for his book *Underground Railroad*.

Another Pulitzer Prize–winning resident was John Steinbeck, arguably Sag Harbor's most famous inhabitant. In his novels, Steinbeck identifies with the common man, and when he first came to Sag Harbor in 1953, he found a populace that embodied the everyman spirit found in his writings.

Steinbeck was living here when he wrote *The Winter of Our Discontent*, a novel purportedly based on the citizenry of Sag Harbor. At one point in the book, its protagonist, Ethan Allen Hawley, a descendent of a prominent whaling family who now works at the local supermarket, is asked by his two children to go to the nearby movies—which could only be the Sag Harbor Cinema.

Change is inevitable and lamentations about it are on full display in the novel where Ethan speaks of the way things used to be—before the souvenir shops and restaurants for tourists. It's a sentiment that is familiar in Sag Harbor and one that has pitted locals against newcomers for generations. As

Sag Harbor Parades
COURTESY OF
ELIZABETH GLASGOW

the newcomers, in turn, become the locals, the sentiment shifts again to the even newer-comers in a timeless dance of "let's make sure it stays the same."

Despite the arrival of more upscale shops and restaurants, several mom-and-pop businesses still function as the anchor for Main Street and they hang on fiercely in the face of an uncertain economy, shifting demographics and long winters. The devastating fire has made many nervous about what will come next.

But tradition is on their side.

Every Memorial Day, Sag Harbor holds a parade on Main Street to honor those who have died in battle, and the sidewalk in front of the cinema has traditionally been the focal point of the parade route. It's where members of the Sag Harbor Community Band take up position and, in their white shirts and red trousers, they sit on folding chairs playing rousing Sousa numbers until the line of marchers approaches. Then the band falls

Every Memorial Day the Sag Harbor Community Band plays in front of the theater.
COURTESY OF THE SAG HARBOR COMMUNITY BAND

silent while a lone trumpeter offers a somber rendition of Taps, followed by a 21-gun salute.

Even in the absence of the theater—which one person recently likened to a missing tooth on Main Street—the Memorial Day parade will be held again this year and the year after as well, and the community band will play on.

The movie theater was one of those old-time businesses that helped cement the foundation of Main Street. It was also the latest of seven theaters that had entertained Sag Harbor since the first silent pictures hit screens at the dawn of the twentieth century.

Many residents of Sag Harbor are already hard at work engineering how the eighth theater might rise from the ashes.

Though the task ahead looms large, Sag Harbor is certainly a village that understands adversity and throughout history, its residents have persevered time and time again. Hopes are high that they'll do so again—working together so that Sag Harbor's namesake beacon shines once more.

Oil on canvas
COURTESY OF MICHAEL COLEMAN

PART ONE
THE EARLY DAYS

1907-1935

THE ATHENEUM

The very first venue to ever screen a movie in Sag Harbor was not a cinema, but rather a playhouse and vaudevillian theater.

The Atheneum sat at the corner of Union and Church Streets— in what is now St. Andrew's Church parking lot—where it presented professionally produced plays by traveling theater companies, as well as amateur productions by Sag Harbor residents and local civic groups.

Though the Atheneum offered a range of performances and activities that made it a true community center in the very real sense, the building began life as a house of worship.

Vintage photo of the
Atheneum from 1905
COURTESY OF THE SAG HARBOR
HISTORICAL SOCIETY

Thanksgiving Pilgrim play at the Atheneum
COURTESY OF THE SAG HARBOR HISTORICAL SOCIETY

Originally situated at the northeast corner of Sage and Church Streets, it was built in 1817 by the Presbyterians who used it for services until 1844, when the congregation moved to the Old Whalers Church—its new imposing home a block away on Union Street.

At that point, the Presbyterians leased their old church to the Episcopalians who were in need of a larger building for their own congregation. Two years later, the Episcopalians bought the church and renovated it to their liking. But in 1880, they decided to build a new church on East Union Street. The old building was sold again in 1881—this time to Wamponamon Lodge #437, otherwise known as the Masons, who transformed it into their meeting place and a hall for entertainment.

Then in 1900, Joseph Fahys & Company purchased the building. The Fahys Watch Case Factory had operated in Sag Harbor since the early 1880s, and its owners were not so much interested in the structure as they were the land beneath, which they wanted to expand their factory.

So in 1903, the company moved the building one block south, to the corner of Church and Union Streets. This is where its life as the Atheneum, a full-fledged community center and theater, really began. Prior to the building's arrival at the new site, a basement was constructed complete with a gym, a bowling alley, bathrooms, dressing rooms, and a furnace room. The building itself received a complete overhaul with the addition of an auditorium that could seat 500, a stage, and a box office. Upstairs, the Masons still had their lodge.

In November 1903, the newly minted Atheneum was complete and the Ladies Village Improvement Society hosted a ball to celebrate the opening. In the years that followed, dances, basketball games, lectures, and all sorts of vaudevillian and musical entertainment offerings found a home at the Atheneum.

As did the movies.

In 1907, the Atheneum showed an experimental silent film, the first known screening of a movie in Sag Harbor. In the years that followed, movies became a more frequent offering at the Atheneum. With the advent of new technology, it may have been that films were much less trouble for the management than live performers were, since films didn't talk back—especially the silents.

This became evident in the Atheneum's negotiations with the Trahern Stock Company. The acting troupe, with 11 actors and a full 10-piece orchestra, was headed by its namesake, Al Trahern, and frequently came to Sag Harbor to perform at the Atheneum.

But in September 1908, Al Trahern went head-to-head with "the powers that be" at the Atheneum over commission.

In a lively exchange of letters published in the newspaper, Mr. Trahern

THE EARLY DAYS · 1907–1935

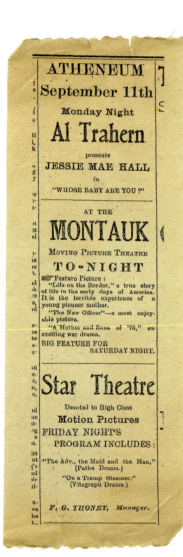

complained about the percentage the Atheneum's manager, Ivan C. Byram, sought to receive from each performance. Apparently, the Atheneum's take had been boosted by five percent from previous engagements. In his letter, an outraged Mr. Trahern explains to disappointed fans why his troupe won't be appearing regularly at the Atheneum that winter as planned.

In his response, Mr. Byram makes clear in no uncertain terms that the rate of the take at the Atheneum remained unchanged, and had, in fact, been lowered in the past to appease Al Trahern:

Twenty-five percent is the lowest percentage ever given any company except yours and I only reduced it for you as you spoke for so many nights.

As for your threats in your letter I don't give a damn.

Yours respectfully,

Ivan C. Byram

Fences apparently were mended between the two because by 1911, Al Trahern's troupe was back at the Atheneum. An advertisement in the paper promised that on Monday, September 11, audiences would see Jessie Mae Hall starring in *Whose Baby Are You?*

But by this point, Jessie and the troupe had strong competition—and it was the movies. In 1911, there were two other theaters operating in Sag Harbor and both advertised the films they were showing in the same issue of the paper. On Washington Street, the Montauk Moving Picture Theatre was screening *Life on the Borde*, a film based on the true story of the early days of America. Meanwhile, the Star Theatre on Main Street was offering a Vitagraph drama called *On a Tramp Steamer.*

With competition all around, the Atheneum picked up the cinematic pace. Frank Sexton took over as manager in 1912, after leaving his partner-

Actor and North Haven resident Robert Edeson and his wife, at the Maud Irving Operetta.
COURTESY OF THE SAG HARBOR HISTORICAL SOCIETY

ship at the Star Theatre, and installed a Simplex Moving Picture Machine in 1915 that allowed the screening of Pathé newsreels, cartoons, and big feature films. In May 1916 the Atheneum screened *Big Jim Garrity* starring Robert Edeson, who appeared in person at the venue in conjunction with the screening.

But the Atheneum remained a theater for live entertainment as well. In the 1920s, the Leiter Light Opera Company came to town, as did the Fennelly Players who performed an evening of sketches. Local groups like the American Legion Chelberg and Battle Post 388 also presented vaudeville programs for the community at the Atheneum. *Foiled, by Heck!*—called "an amusing sketch" by the *Sag Harbor Express*—was offered by the Legion in February 1992, featuring Frank Geisler as a farmer and Gurden S. Harris who, with his toothless smile, kept the audience laughing.

By then, the Atheneum's days were numbered. At 10:10 a.m. on the morning of April 30, 1924, a fire was discovered in the basement furnace room, and within minutes, the roofs of 15 nearby houses and stores had

THE EARLY DAYS · 1907–1935

caught on fire due to burning embers, some of which traveled nearly a quarter of a mile.

Newspaper reports indicate it might have been one of the worst fires in Sag Harbor history had the local firefighters not been successful in their efforts to drench neighboring buildings in order to keep the flames from spreading further.

Oddly enough, one of the Sag Harbor homes that caught fire belonged to Antone Basile who, several hours earlier, had alerted authorities to a burning building in Flanders that he and his wife had discovered while driving home from Riverhead.

Both the building in Flanders and the Atheneum were totally destroyed by their respective fires that day. On the third floor of the Atheneum were rooms where the Foresters, Companions of the Forest, Shepherds of America, and the Knights of Columbus all held their meetings. The lodges lost all of their paraphernalia in the fire.

At the time of the Atheneum's demise in 1924, both the Montauk and the Star Theatres were long gone and only one other theater was operating in Sag Harbor—The Elite at 90 Main Street, an address that would ultimately be home to a total of four movie houses over the course of 101 years, including the Sag Harbor Cinema.

BURNING DOWN THE HOUSE

"We used to go to the Atheneum Theatre. In those days it was like Guild Hall is today, but not as elegant.

"One time, I remember when they were having a benefit and I had just come home. I had been studying dancing in New York City all winter and was asked to do a dance. Someone played the violin and someone else sang. I decided to do an Oriental dance, which I had rehearsed at school. I had a dress, the bra was of gold cloth, and I had briefs, as they called them in those days. They were shorts in gold cloth, and the skirt was long black chiffon, which was banded in gold. While we were practicing I said, 'Turn out the footlights when I come out to dance.' Well, they didn't turn out the footlights, and when I came out to dance, the footlights practically took my skin right off me. This was 79 years ago. That night, the Atheneum burned down, and I never lived it down. They all said that I set the Atheneum on fire."

Anita Anderson rehearsing her Oriental dance.
COURTESY OF THE SAG HARBOR HISTORICAL SOCIETY

Anita M. S. Anderson died April 7, 2005 at the age of 100.
From *Sag Harbor Voices*, edited by Nina Tobier

MONTAUK MOVING PICTURE THEATRE

Located on Washington Street across from the Bulova Watchcase Factory (then operated by Joseph Fahys & Company), this popular film theater opened in 1908. It must have been a welcome outlet for the hard-working populace of Sag Harbor, because its success was almost immediate

Owned by John Carroll and Edward Welsh, the theater was managed by F. C. Thonet and it opened shortly after the Atheneum screened its experimental film. The new medium caught on quickly and business was apparently booming, because in 1909, just a year after opening, the village granted permission for a 20-foot brick extension to be added to the back of the theater.

The next decade gave rise to the creation of regional film exhibition chains and names that are still familiar today—including Loew's in New York. These theaters ultimately became the end product of the vertically integrated film industry that dominated from the 1920s to 1940s.

But in Sag Harbor in the 1910s, the Montauk Moving Picture Theatre, like the Atheneum and the nearby Star, didn't solely rely on films for programming. Instead, the theater balanced the bill by offering a combination of both movies and live entertainment.

And sometimes it offered a unique melding of the two.

In the fall of 1910, Leo Ormond, a top New York tenor, was retained on contract to sing "illustrated songs" twice daily at the Montauk accompanied by a local pianist referred to only as "Mrs. VanHoughton."

Performers like Ormond were vital to theaters like the Montauk. Sound technology for movies was still years away, so theater owners had to get creative with the lineup. Illustrated songs did just that. They were not movies, but rather a series of slides that were projected on screen while the live singer or a pianist offered musical accompaniment.

Movie posters plastered the walls of the Arsenal, located at Union and Madison Streets next to the old burial grounds.
PHOTO BY WILLIAM WALLACE TOOKER, FROM THE KEVIN J. McCANN COLLECTION.

In an editorial printed in its December 12, 1908 issue, *The Moving Picture World*, a trade journal for the American film industry, expounded on the art of pulling off a successful illustrated song:

> The singer should be as good as can be afforded. Of course, it is understood that the audiences that attend moving picture shows are not looking for Pattis or Carusos, but, after all, singers can be obtained who have good voices and who can interpret a song reasonably well. Inasmuch as the songs are sung in the dark the action of the singer makes little difference. The voice and the slides should both be good.

The Montauk also continued to book vaudevillian acts and other traveling troupes that showed up from time to time to entertain the masses. If things were going well, these troupes might stick around for a while.

THE EARLY DAYS · 1907–1935

For example, on September 19, 1911, a local newspaper raved about the performance of Hilda Lee, age 5, who sang "Under the Yum Yum Tree" at the Montauk. She was part of a traveling family troupe and it was noted that the Lees were set to be at the Montauk for an indefinite engagement, so chances were good that audiences would have an opportunity to hear little Hilda sing again.

Some of the performances on offer in those early years of cinema had the flavor of Coney Island sideshow attractions. Even in tiny Sag Harbor, great extravaganzas and impressive feats of skill or daring were the order of the day. The same week that little Hilda wowed the crowd, a performer named "Sampson the Great" gave an exhibition of strength in front of the Montauk Moving Picture Theatre by holding a team of horses pulling in opposite directions. Afterwards, he performed inside the theater, and in the week ahead, he promised to "break a 10 inch spike between his teeth and bend a one inch bar of iron and do other feats of strength."

As if an afterthought, the columnist added, "The usual program of fine pictures will also be shown."

One of the films that did deserve a great deal of attention when it screened at the Montauk in 1911 was *Vanity Fair*, based on the novel by William Makepeace Thackeray. It was produced and directed by Charles Kent for the Vitagraph Company, and Robert Tabor, a Sag Harbor native and former resident, had a small part as an aide-de-camp in the film.

While perhaps not the most memorable role, Tabor's appearance in *Vanity Fair* may have been the first example of a Sag Harbor boy finding his way onto the silver screen.

No matter how exciting the movie or the live performer, in the days before air-conditioning a hot, dark, and stuffy theater was likely the last place audiences wanted to be on a summer evening. One of the innovative techniques that the Montauk and theaters around the country employed to keep audiences coming in warm months was the use of an airdome.

An airdome was a fancy term for an open-air movie theater. Think of it as the precurser to the drive-in, but without the cars. In a 1913 report on the industry by David S. Hulfish, the airdome is described as a yard enclosed by an 8 to 10 foot high fence or canvas wall. Inside the yard, "a projection house is built at one end, and a picture screen of usual theater dimension is placed at the other end." Chairs were arranged in front of the screen, and a platform could be added for vaudeville performances as well as a refreshment area for musicians to play behind the screen.

The Montauk Moving Picture Theatre's airdome was said to have been located on Main Street. Though the exact location is not known, Mashashimuet Park at Jermain Avenue and Main Street may be a good guess.

When cooler weather arrived with fall, the airdrome shut down and audiences returned to the Montauk's permanent home on Washington Street. At the end of summer in September 1911, patrons learned they had something new to look forward to in the season ahead at the theater—heat. Newspaper articles promised that a hot air furnace would soon be installed at the Montauk.

Despite its popularity, the Montauk Moving Picture Theatre was short-lived, as was one of its owners. On April 1, 1911, John Carroll died and the theater closed for a week out of a show of respect. In his will, Carroll instructed his executor, James J. Brooks, to sell his share of the theater and airdome business for not less than $1,000 and give the proceeds to his siblings, while "the piano and music, he gives to his two sisters."

The Montauk Moving Picture Theatre closed its doors for good in 1912 after four years of operation.

Unfortunately, no photographs of the Montauk have been found.

Yes, they shot it here . . .
THE BONDMAN, 1916

This silent adaptation of Hail Caine's 1890 novel was released by Fox during the 1915-1916 movie season. It starred William Farnum and Doris Woolridge and told the story of Jason Orry, the bondman of the Isle of Man. Because of an injustice to his mother, Jason vows revenge against Sunlocks (played by Harry Spingler), a half brother he doesn't know whom he chases to Iceland. There, they both fall in love with the same woman.

Farnum was a summer resident of the Actor's Colony in North Haven where many famous actors had summer homes beginning in the early 1900s. According to historian Dorothy Zaykowski, the film production crew constructed a fishing village complete with cottages for the shoot, while a bridge was built over a stream near the ferry slip at the top of North Haven. Several locals had parts as extras in the film.

Actor William Farnum

THE STAR

Like the Montauk Moving Picture Theatre, the Star Theatre was a venue for vaudeville performances and film. It opened in 1909, just a year after the Montauk, and could seat 300 people. Located on the west side of Main Street a few doors north of what is now the IGA, it sat between Blaiklock's Garage and Shapiro's Restaurant. Managed by the team of Ryland and Roberts, many people wondered if a town as small as Sag Harbor could support two theaters, as well as the Atheneum, which was still going strong. But it appeared there was enough theatrical and cinematic demand to go around, and not long after opening, the Star was described as "a comfortable little theater" with lots of fine programs every night of the week.

The theater billed itself as "Devoted to High Class Motion Pictures." A newspaper ad for the Star from September 1911 promoted a screening of *The Ad, the Maid and the Man*, an offering by the French company Pathé, a major film equipment and production company. In the early 1900s both Vitagraph and Pathé produced newsreels that became standard cinema fare and ran prior to the main attractions.

In 1912, a local businessman named George Kiernan (whose great granddaughter still lives in Sag Harbor) got into the movie business by purchasing the Star Theatre. Soon, Edward Walsh of the Montauk Moving Picture Theatre attempted to lease the Star from Kiernan. But the deal fell through, so Walsh shut down the Montauk and left town to open a new theater in Southampton.

Fire has never been a stranger on Main Street, and like many buildings in Sag Harbor, the Star fell victim to one. In May 1913, a blaze destroyed the theater's electrical powerhouse. This was a hazard of the era, and when it came to cinema fires, often the film itself was to blame. The nitrate film used in the early twentieth century was sensitive to humidity, static electricity, friction, light, and heat—all things that it would encounter during its journey through an electric projector and past a hot lamp.

Projection booths were notoriously hazardous places to work. As movies increased in length, so did the risk. Longer films required the use of two projectors, and projectionists would jump from one machine to the other in order to ensure the next reel was ready to go when the time came. Film did catch fire quite easily, sometimes with disastrous consequences, as portrayed in the 1988 feature, *Cinema Paradiso*.

But the Star's fire was not quite as serious as that, and the theater was closed for just a few weeks due to the blaze. When it reopened, it had a new fireproof booth to protect audience members. The projectionists, however, were still on their own.

In 1915, M. Tanneberg took over management of the Star from Kiernan, and he put in place a contract with World Film Corporation, which included the theatrical interests of the Shuberts and William A. Brady, both Broadway producers. As a result, the cinema began showing Broadway plays that had been made into films at the reasonable price of 15 cents (10 cents for children). On Saturday nights Charlie Chaplin films were featured, and in June 1915 another local appeared on-screen in Sag Harbor—Robert Edeson who starred in Fox Film Corporation's *The Girl I Left Behind Me*. Finally in November 1923, the Star ceased operation and Kiernan sold the building to a man named Morris Meyer.

But George Kiernan wasn't quite done with the movies yet.

FANNIE TUNISON:
Sag Harbor's sideshow seamstress

Fannie Tunison
COURTESY JACK YOUNGS

One of Sag Harbor's most intriguing residents during the vaudeville era garnered quite a bit of fame on the stage, and though there is no evidence she ever performed locally, her unique skill set was legendary.

Her name was Fannie W. Tunison. Born in 1870, Fannie lived with her parents in a tiny house on Hampton Street. As an infant she became paralyzed from the neck down, but rather than being a burden on her family, as a young woman she developed amazing skills as a seamstress and ended up supporting them all.

Her father, Abraham Tunison, built a custom work-bench and chair with a strap that held her upright and, using only her mouth and tongue, Fannie was able to thread needles, paint, draw, write, string beads, sew, embroider, and even manage scissors. Fannie exhibited and sold her work at fairs and ultimately garnered national attention with her talents, which included card reading and fortune telling.

On July 27, 1902, the *New York Times* reported in its Vaudeville and Concert Programs, "After undergoing extensive alterations, Huber's Fourteenth Street Museum throws open its doors to the public to-morrow. For the opening week the management presents Fannie Tunison, the Sag Harbor woman who, deprived of the use of her arms and feet, executes by lip and mouth, specimens of painting, drawing, needlework, and sewing."

Fannie Tunison died in 1944 at 74. She is buried in Sag Harbor's Oakland Cemetery. Her work-table and chair are in the collection of the Sag Harbor Historical Society.

GEORGE'S THEATRE

With his next theater, George Kiernan kept to the west side of Main Street, but he moved south a bit and bought the Hennigar property opposite Washington Street. He tore the building down, brought in the Corwin Brothers of North Haven to construct a new one, and, in October 1915, opened George's Theatre to the public.

This was the first of four theaters to occupy 90 Main Street over the next 101 years, and many residents were scandalized—not because of the films that Kiernan showed, but because he had the audacity to violate blue laws by opening the theater on Sundays.

Still, that apparently didn't dissuade moviegoers or other patrons. In 1916, George's Theatre was the site of a men's meeting held at 3 p.m. on a Sunday afternoon. The newspaper encouraged people to "Go and hear Mr. Pugsley, a well-learned propounder of truths" . . . whatever those may be.

At some point in his tenure at 90 Main Street, George Kiernan purchased a saloon from S. Rosenthal to complete his creation of a large Main Street frontage that purportedly ran from George's Theatre to Heller's Alley.

In 1917, Dr. G. C. McKay took over management of George's Theatre and upped the ante by bringing in new machinery and a higher class of entertainment than had been there prior. In addition to up-market vaudeville acts, the theater hosted the trio of Charles F. Van, Aurelia Clark, and James M. Cole, who appeared in the musical comedy *The New King of Tramps*. Music was provide by Cole's Red Hussar Concert Band and Orchestra.

In truth, there isn't a lot of historic information to be found about the films that were screened at George's Theatre in the mid to late teens. But it was a difficult time in history.

In *The History of Motion Pictures* by Maurice Bardèche and Robert Brasillach, the authors write, "The end of the war coincided with a crisis in

The Sag Harbor Armistice Parade 1918
COURTESY OF THE SAG HARBOR
HISTORICAL SOCIETY

Yes, they shot it here...
BACK HOME AND BROKE, 1922

This comedy silent film was written by George Ade and J. Clarkson Miller, based on Ade's play. It was shot in Sag Harbor by the Famous Players Lasky Corporation and directed by Alfred E. Green. The stars included Thomas Meighan, Lila Lee, Frederick Burton, Cyril Ring, Charles S. Abbe, Florence Dixon, and Gertrude Quinlan. The film was released on December 24, 1922, by Paramount Pictures.

The plot follows the trials and tribulations of Tom Redding (Meighan) after his wealthy father dies leaving him nothing but debt. Determined to get out of the red, Tom heads west where he strikes it rich in oil. He hatches a plan to return to his hometown under the guise of being broke to get even with his former friends who deserted him when he was down on his luck.

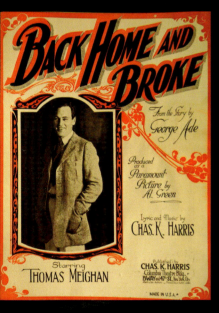

Poster from the release of *Back Home and Broke*.
COURTESY OF JOE MARKOWSKI

According to historian Dorothy Zaykowski, when location manager Arthur Cozine found Sag Harbor he felt it was the perfect setting for *Back Home and Broke*. During the shooting, the cast stayed at rooming houses throughout the village. Many Main Street buildings could be seen in the final film and a number of locals had parts in a parade scene. The film had its first Long Island showing at the Elite Theatre. In June 1933, it was re-released and played at Glynne's Sag Harbor Theatre and an orchestra was hired to provide accompaniment for the silent film.

The cast of *Back Home and Broke* at the Sag Harbor Yacht Club in 1922.
COURTESY OF JOE MARKOWSKI

Vintage postcard of Sag Harbor circa 1910. The low, flat-roofed building to the left of the white canopy was to become the site of George's Theatre, and the start of a 101 year run of movie houses at 90 Main Street.

the American film industry. Most of the companies had undergone radical changes during 1918. Towards the end of that year the influenza epidemic swept the country; many of the cinemas closed, and it was difficult to get anyone to rent a film."

As the flu spread across the nation, health officials in many municipalities ordered the closing of movie theaters, schools, churches, or other places where large groups would gather—even funerals. In Los Angeles, movie theaters were shut down for seven weeks, which led to great financial hardship. But in New York no closures were issued at all.

The flu pandemic killed 50 million people worldwide. While there's no evidence that there was an official quarantine in Sag Harbor prohibiting people from going to the theater, the National Association of the Motion Picture Industry called for a four-week shutdown of film production at the time, not because of the flu itself, but in order to avoid the economic chaos producers felt would result by trying to release new films while so many theaters were under quarantine.

Whatever the case, by 1919, George's Theatre was gone, and the venue had changed both ownership and name.

THE ELITE

The Elite was the second movie house to occupy 90 Main Street in Sag Harbor. Owned by Marshall Seaton, it opened in October 1919 and had an impressive 700 seats on the main floor with another 300 in a newly built balcony. Also new was a Wurlitzer Orchestra organ, which was touted as a strong attraction at the Elite.

The first feature to be shown at the Elite was *His Majesty, the American*. It also happened to be the first film released by United Artists, which was founded in 1919 by D. W. Griffith, Charlie Chaplin, Mary Pickford, and Douglas Fairbanks. The film was directed by Victor Fleming who, in 1939, also directed both *The Wizard of Oz* and *Gone With the Wind*, and it had a budget of $300,000. *His Majesty, the American* starred Fairbanks, a popular swashbuckling actor of the silent era.

As a cinema owner in tiny Sag Harbor, Seaton understood the value of good marketing and public relations. To mark the theater's first anniversary,

The original Elite Theatre
Reprinted from *Sag Harbor In the Land of the Sunrise Trail: 1707–1927*
COURTESY OF JOE MARKOWSKI

Vintage photo showing a billboard for the Elite Theatre on the side of Ballen's hardware store at the corner of Washington Street and Main.

the Elite partnered with Mashashimuet Park to offer movies for children every Friday night.

And movies were getting more elaborate and expensive to make. In a March 1922 advertisement in the *Sag Harbor Express*, the Elite promoted the screening of *Theodora*, a film about a former slave girl who becomes Empress

Firemen turning up Washington Street in front of the Elite Theatre to the old Sag Harbor firehouse, 1928.
COURTESY OF THE SAG HARBOR HISTORICAL SOCIETY

Yes, they shot it here . . .
NO MAN OF HER OWN, 1932

Clark Gable and Carole Lombard starred in this film from Paramount Studios. Location scouts spent three days on Long Island before deciding on Sag Harbor for the shoot. In the film, Clark Gable plays Babe Stewart, a card cheat who is on the lam. Carole Lombard plays Connie Randall, a lonely librarian who marries Babe after a coin flip. After learning the truth of his con man ways, there are some rough patches, but the two remained committed to one another.

The film was shown at Glynne's Sag Harbor Theatre on March 8, 1933, much to the delight of residents who recognized many of the locations and extras. A few years after *No Man of Her Own*, Gable and Lombard got married in real life—it's said that they fell in love while working on the film in Sag Harbor.

Opening scene entering Sag Harbor from *No Man of Her Own*,

It was a town of moviegoers...

From the diaries of Ethel Youngs, 1927

COURTESY OF JACK YOUNGS

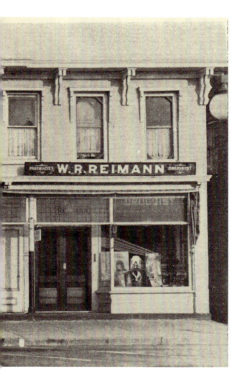

Reimann's Drugstore, where movie tickets could be bought.
COURTESY OF JOE MARKOWSKI

of Rome. The film cost an astounding $3 million to make and included a cast of 25,000.

"Forty lions were turned loose into a crowded arena among thousands of people—to satisfy the whim of a love mad woman," read the advertisement.

Still, like many of the earlier theaters in Sag Harbor, the Elite wasn't entirely devoted to motion pictures. When Seaton retired in January 1924, Samuel Rosenthal took over its management. He made several improvements to the theater, including relocation of the ticket office, the addition of three new chandeliers, and some new interior décor. Curiously, he also removed the first row of seats and leveled the floor so that the area could be used as a basketball court and dance floor.

And the vaudevilles were still alive and well. In August 1926, news reports indicated that Alice Rector, a dancer on the traveling circuit who was summering in Sag Harbor, had agreed to appear in a vaudeville show at the Elite along with a group of child entertainers and Ed Massy, the "Bad Boy from a Good Family."

A movie was also on the bill: *The Girl from Montmartre*.

In 1927, the theater changed hands and was bought by Mike Glynne, who gave it his name.

GLYNNE'S SAG HARBOR THEATRE

When Mike Glynne bought the Elite Theatre at 90 Main Street in September 1927, he was building on a mini-empire—the Sag Harbor venue was added to a chain of theaters that he owned across eastern Long Island, including in Patchogue, Bay Shore, Southampton, and Greenport.

He was rumored to have paid between $35,000 and $40,000 for the property and changed the name to Glynne's Sag Harbor Theatre. It was the third theater to operate on the site and Mike Glynne settled into a new era as a cinema proprietor—one in which the moving pictures had begun to speak up.

Up until the 1920s, because they were silent, movies often took second billing to live vaudeville shows. Then, in 1926, Western Electric developed Vitaphone's new sound-on-disc system. It didn't play dialogue, per se, but offered music and sound effects that were recorded on a wax record and synchronized with the projector.

Warner Brothers was the first studio to use the system with its 1926 film *Don Juan* starring John Barrymore that was directed by Alan Crosland. Despite the success of the film, many studios remained skeptical about the technology, willing to bet that sound movies would never replace the silents.

But the premiere of *The Jazz Singer* in New York on October 6, 1927 changed everything. This film was also released by Warner Brothers and directed by Alan Crosland, and it starred Al Jolson. It was the first feature-length film with talking sequences.

It would be another two years, however, until the talkies found their way to Sag Harbor. On October 13, 1929, Glynne's Sag Harbor Theatre made history with its screening of *Kitty*, the first sound feature to be shown on the East End. It was a British drama and love story set during World War I, but the sound had to be recorded at RKO studios in New York because the technology in England was not yet up to par.

As a theater owner, Mike Glynne obviously had faith in the future of the medium because in September 1930, he took a big leap by purchasing a new RCA Sound System. The theater had to close down for six weeks while it was installed.

The advent of sound technology may have been good news for the movies and theater owners, but it spelled doom for vaudeville. No longer were live acts the primary draw at theaters that also showed films. Many silent film actors were unable to make the transition—especially those with heavy foreign accents or unpleasant speaking voices.

Even Douglas Fairbanks, Hollywood royalty and one of the biggest stars of the 1910s and 1920s, couldn't make the switch. He made his final film, *The Private Life of Don Juan*, in 1934 and died just five years later at the age of 56.

But in the 1930s, Mike Glynne and his chain of movie theaters was going strong. In 1932, he opened his most spectacular cinema of them all— Glynne's Southampton Theatre, which was reportedly the most impressive on the East End. Though the building survives to this day, it has been renovated and carved up into four separate cinemas and retains none of its original glamour.

PART TWO

FROM SILENTS TO CINEMASCOPE

1936–1978

In June 1936, Prudential Playhouses, Inc. opened the Sag Harbor Theatre at 90 Main Street. The old Elite auditorium had been demolished to make way for a new a two-story, three-bay fireproof cinema box made of steel and concrete—which may explain why that portion of the cinema was largely intact after the 2016 fire.

Built in just nine weeks, the Sag Harbor Theatre was billed in the *Sag Harbor Express* as the newest of the chain of Suffolk County movie theaters operated by the Prudential Long Island Theatres, Inc. The story went on to note "the new Sag Harbor Theatre, although not the largest, will be one of the finest playhouses on Long Island. The theatre, which will seat 516 persons, will be equipped with the best sound and project apparatus obtainable, comfortable chairs, luxurious carpets, and delightful rest rooms, all set in a harmony of blended lighting and harmonious color."

The new cinema was reported to cost $25,000 and it was the work of famed theater designer John Eberson. Even today, it's pretty remarkable to think that someone of Eberson's caliber designed the modest movie house in Sag Harbor. Throughout the 1920s, Eberson had built his reputation by creating some of the grandest movie theaters in the United States. Known as "atmospherics," his theaters were huge, some could seat more than 3,000 people, and they were designed to evoke Spanish courtyards, Moorish palaces, or Italian villas. His Palace Theatre in Marion, Ohio, built in 1928, even had low-voltage lighting in the ceiling to mimic stars and a machine that simulated moving clouds.

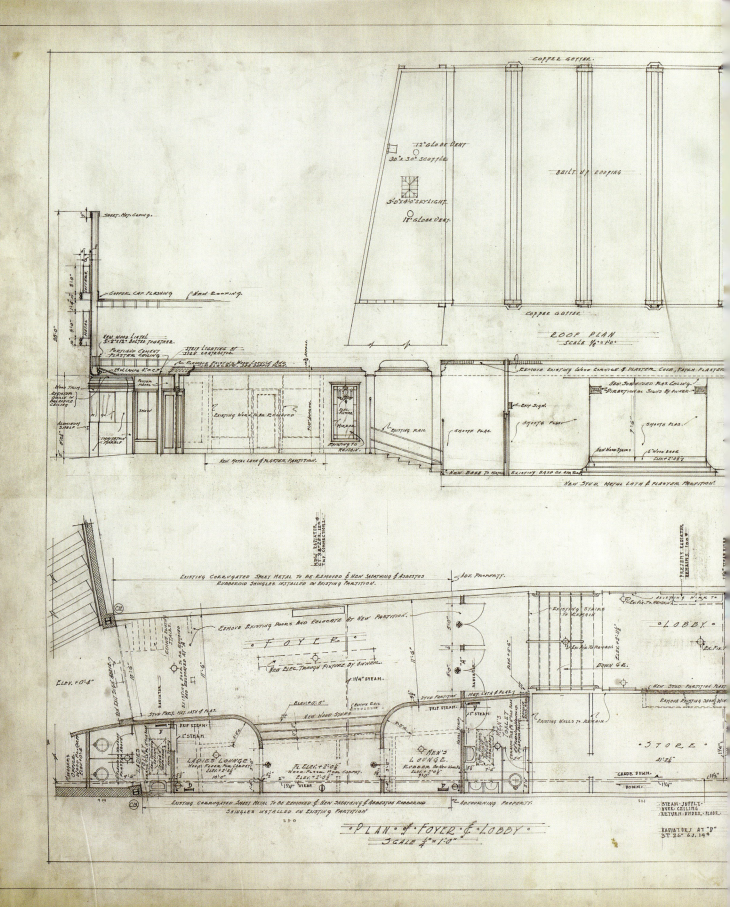

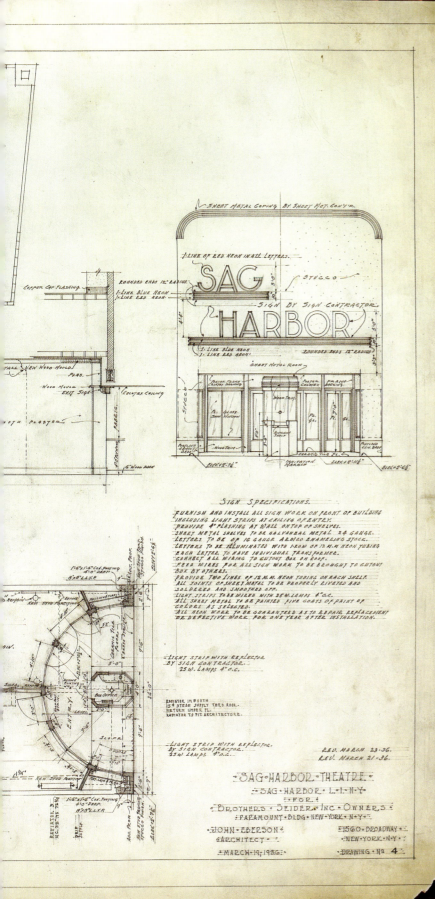

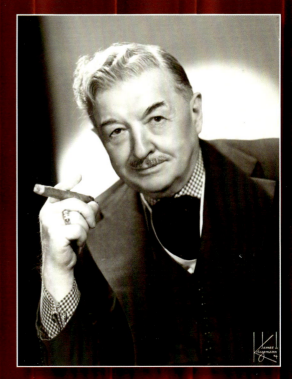

John Eberson, the "Valentino of cinema design."
COURTESY OF THE THEATRE HISTORICAL SOCIETY OF AMERICA

Architect John Eberson's original rendering for the Sag Harbor Theatre.
COURTESY OF THE WOLFSONIAN–FIU

"My mom used to sing in the Sweet Adelines [a cappella group]. They practiced there. The theater was built in 1935 or 1936—my dad was born in 1925, so he was 10 when it was built. My family on the Cullum side was from Greenport and Shelter Island. The photographs are of my grandfather Raymond, of R. Cullum and Sons Contractor, building the theater."

MEMORIES OF DELL CULLUM

COURTESY OF DELL CULLUM HISTORICAL PHOTO COLLECTION / IMAGINATIONNATURE.COM

"When the theater burned down, someone took a picture of one of the walls that had been hidden behind a wall. In a window filled in with cinder blocks, one of the bricks has 1935 written on it."

MEMORIES OF DELL CULLUM

Gerry Mallow photographing the original 1935 cinder block.

Vintage photo showing the original outdoor ticket booth.
COURTESY OF JOE MARKOWSKI

But by the early 1930s, the Depression was on and economics had changed drastically. Hopes for a modern, bright, and streamlined future dominated the '30s and were embodied in art deco design that found its way into everything from skyscrapers and trains to cars and appliances.

Eberson's 1930s theater designs were far more understated than the atmospherics had been. By this time, his son Drew had joined him in the business and together they became known for their art deco theater designs—among them the Sag Harbor Theatre.

With fewer than 600 seats, a plain façade, and simple lines, Sag Harbor Theatre was built on a scale of economy that fit well in the small village. Eberson's business model was based on standardization—his art deco theater designs had four floor plans that could be customized based on seating,

The iconic theater sign
COURTESY OF BOB WEINSTEIN

volume, and décor. He also relied on prefabricated elements assembled on site, which made his model even more economical for theater owners.

Another major change in theaters of the era that was on full display at the Sag Harbor Theatre was the use of the lobby area. The wide-open gathering spaces that defined opera movie palaces in the 1920s were gone. Now those spaces were given over to the selling of concessions—an important new income producer in the 1930s.

Lobbies became home to glass candy cases and machines that dispensed popcorn. Even into the 1950s and 1960s, Sag Harbor residents remember getting their popcorn from an automated machine at the theater and paying a penny to buy a paper cup for water.

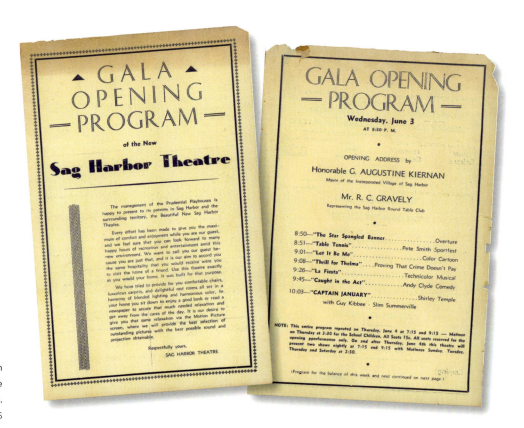

The orignal program from opening night of the Sag Harbor Theatre, 1936.
COURTESY OF JACK YOUNGS

EXPRESS-NEWS & CORRECTOR, THURS., MAY 28, 1936

Congratulations and Best Wishes to the
New SAG HARBOR THEATRE

COMPLIMENTS OF

Sag Harbor Market
MOESCHLE and HEINRICHS
Props.

REMEMBER
The Graduate and June Bride
with Watches, Jewelry and
Silverware.

C. E. FRITTS
Jeweler and Optometrist
Sag Harbor, N. Y.   Phone 133

HANSEN'S
Ben Franklin Stores
5c   10c $1.00   Merchandise

Sag Harbor   Southampton

Sag Harbor Liquor Store
COMPLETE LINE
of Domestic and Imported Liquors
L. B. Nichols   Lic. No. L-1245

Congratulations

Sag Harbor Round Table Club

COMPLIMENTS OF

THE IDEAL CASH STORE

Gala Opening Performance
Wed., June 3 at 8:30 p.m.

ALL SEATS RESERVED ON SALE ONE WEEK IN ADVANCE

Short subjects on this program

Table Tennis
Let It Be Me
Thrill for Thelma
La Fiesta
Caught in the Act

Little Lady of the Lighthouse

Shirley **TEMPLE** in "**Captain January**"
WITH
GUY KIBBEE
Slim SUMMERVILLE
JUNE LANG
BUDDY EBSEN
SARA HADEN
20th Century-Fox Picture

Entire Program also Playing Thurs. June 4
Matinee - Night

THIS THEATRE WILL BE OPEN EVERY DAY WITH MATINEES SUN, TUES. THUR., SAT
TWO COMPLETE SHOWS EVERY NIGHT AT 7:15 - 9:15

SUN. and MON June 7 and 8

ADDED SHORTS

UNDER TWO FLAGS
Claudette Colbert finds her perfect screen sweetheart at last in Ronald Colman

MATINEE SUNDAY 2:30

FRI. and SAT. June 5 and 6

TWO FEATURES

THE GREATEST Charlie CHAPLIN **MODERN TIMES**
Released thru United Artists — Paulette Goddard

AND
A ROMANCE OF TODAY'S YOUTH

Janet GAYNOR Robert TAYLOR
"**SMALL TOWN GIRL**"

TWO FEATURES

Wed. and Thurs., June 10 and 11
Clark Gable - Myrna Loy
Jean Harlow
in
Wife Versus Secretary

TUES., June 9:- One Day Only
Special School Matinee at 3:45
in
The Country Doctor
with Jean Hersholt

ALL SEATS RESERVED FOR OPENING NIGHT'S PERFORMANCE
On Sale One Week in Advance

AFTER THE SHOW
Visit
Our Fountain
We Make Fountain Drinks and Dishes
That Make Friends

SAG HARBOR CANDY KITCHEN and RESTAURANT

Fordam & Lyons
ELECTRICIANS
Sag Harbor L. I.   Phone 299

SPITZ'S Radio AND Appliance Shop
KELVINATOR REFRIGERATORS
Ask about our easy Budget Plan
Main St.   Phone 159   Sag Harbor

E. C. KEATING MEN'S SHOP

Located in the new THEATRE BUILDING

SCHIAVONI'S
Fresh Fruits and Vegetables
Delicatessen
and
Fancy Groceries
Free Delivery   Tel. 472

COMPLIMENTS OF

PECONIC BANK

The PIERSON CANDY SHOP & RESTAURANT
EXCLUSIVE AGENT
For
Louis Sherry
Ice Cream

AFTER THE SHOW
VISIT
The Municipal Bar and Grill

> "Let us all take a lesson from their faith and pull together just as we've done to get this new theatre."

By the 1930s, it was also possible to create glowing neon colors in a range of hues. Of course, the key art deco element of the Sag Harbor Theatre was that iconic marquee of red and blue which remained its defining feature for the next eight decades.

On Wednesday, June 3, 1936, at 8:30 p.m., the new Sag Harbor Theatre opened its doors for the first time to great fanfare. A capacity crowd turned out to hear speeches by Mayor G. Augustine Kiernan (not the same Kiernan who owned George's Theater), and R. C. Graveley of the Sag Harbor Round Table Club.

The *Sag Harbor Express* of June 4, 1936 documented the occasion: "We should congratulate ourselves, every member of this community, that the Prudential circuit has such confidence in the future of Sag Harbor,' said Mr. Graveley. 'Let us all take a lesson from their faith and pull together, just as we've done to get this new theatre.'"

The two men told the audience that the people of Sag Harbor should "take hope and encouragement from the expression of faith in the future of the village manifest by the Prudential Playhouses Inc. in erecting the new play house."

"This new theatre," said Mayor Kiernan, "is a decided asset to Sag Harbor. All of us should congratulate each other upon its completion."

The opening night performance featured Shirley Temple in *Captain January*. Short subjects on the program included *Table Tennis*, *Let It Be Me*, *Thrill for Thelma*, *La Fiesta*, and *Caught in the Act*. All seats were reserved in advance. Tickets were 40 cents (children, 20 cents). For matinees, the price was 30 cents adults, 15 cents children.

Also showing that weekend was *Modern Times* starring Charlie Chaplin and *Small Town Girl* with Janet Gaynor and Robert Taylor. The theater was open daily with matinees Sunday, Tuesday, Thursday, and Saturday with two complete shows every night at 7:15 and 9:15 p.m.

The Sag Harbor Candy Kitchen and Restaurant, a couple doors away on Main Street, invited guests to come for fountain drinks after the show.

The era of the Sag Harbor Theatre was officially underway.

The lobby of the Sag Harbor Cinema.
COURTESY OF GAIL GALLAGHER

Vintage Sag Harbor

SAG HARBOR THEATRE 1936-1978

With its opening in 1936, the Sag Harbor Theatre quickly became a center for the community in virtually every sense of the word. Through the lean years of the late 1930s and on into the 1940s when war broke out in Europe and the Pacific, the glamorous movie stars and the stories they brought to life on the big screen were surely a welcome escape from the realities of the outside world.

The 1930s and 1940s were also the era of the cliffhangers—those exciting serial films in which the hero would inevitably be left in a precarious and seemingly inescapable position at the end of the episode, his fate unknown until the next installment. Yet somehow, he always managed to escape the following week—an empowering message at a time when so much of the world was out of control. A kid could definitely while away hours getting lost in the drama of it all.

This was also the era of the Movietone newsreels. With their rousing music, authoritative announcers, and upbeat patriotic messages, these short films offered a glimpse of how our boys were doing "over there." World War II was the most well-documented conflict in history and the black and white footage that made it onto cinema screens around the country gave the most up-to-date information on what was happening abroad. For many young women and parents in Sag Harbor, newsreels provided regular updates of boyfriends and sons in the service—and there was always the remote chance of catching a glimpse of a loved one in uniform in one of the newsreels.

Sag Harbor's Singing Sisters

During this era, the theater also sought to take locals away by showing diversions that weren't about Hollywood, but the talents of those in Sag Harbor. Each year, Sacred Heart Academy, the Catholic school in Sag Harbor, held a St. Patrick's Day talent show fundraiser at the theater, and one of the knockout acts that would always take the stage showcased two young sisters who attended the school.

Even today, if you ask residents of a certain age to name the most famous performers to ever come out of Sag Harbor, they'll inevitably say "the Moylan Sisters."

Born in the early 1930s, Marianne and Peggy Joan Moylan grew up on Madison Street and later lived on Main Street near the Whaling Museum. Called the "Cinderellas of Radio," the sisters were known for their amazing harmonizing skills. They never had formal vocal instruction, but were taught to harmonize by their musically inclined father, Joseph Moylan, who worked at Bulova as an engraver.

At the height of their success, their radio show was second only to *The Shadow* in popularity.

FROM SILENTS TO CINEMASCOPE · 1936–1978

the Moylan Sisters in the Harbor

The Moylan Sisters album.

The Moylans sitting outside the corner store at Jermain and Madison Street, 1941.

The Moylans in Sagaponack.

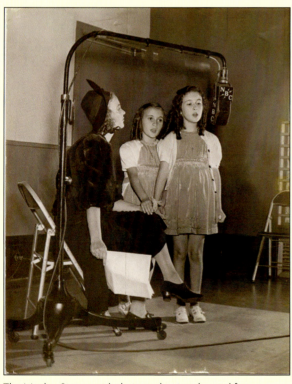

The Moylan Sisters with their mother in rehearsal for their radio show.

The Moylan Sisters' fan picture.

COURTESY OF JACK YOUNGS

The Moylan Sisters appearing at the Sag Harbor Theatre.

The Moylan Sisters on the air.

COURTESY OF MARYELLEN LeCLERC

They were first featured as singers on a radio show called *The Horn and Hardart Children's Hour* and in 1939, Marianne, age 7, and Peggy Joan, age 5, were given a weekly 15-minute network show on NBC Radio in New York. Part of their broadcast involved plugging Thrivo dog food, and every week they'd sing in harmony:

We feed our doggie Thrivo, it's very much alive-o, full of pep and vim.
If you want a peppy pup, you'd better hurry up—buy Thrivo for him.

In December 1936, the Moylans made it to the big screen with their film debut—*Backyard Broadcast*, a two-reel kiddie revue produced by Warner Bros. The film was shown at the Sag Harbor Theatre in conjunction with the main feature, *Cain and Mabel* starring Clark Gable and Marion Davies, and the Moylan Sisters appeared in person during the event.

The sisters made three other short films, and while their perfect pitch and harmony made them stars, their Sag Harbor roots kept them grounded. At the height of their success, their radio show was second only to *The Shadow* in popularity. Though Marianne and Peggy Joan continued to perform through the war years, once they became adults they retired their singing act and settled down to quiet lives.

COURTESY OF THE SAG HARBOR EXPRESS

"I was born in the building next to the cinema. We lived upstairs. My parents opened their store in 1930—Fil Net, ladies clothing.

"The move theater was like my baby sitter. I lived next door, I was there all the time and I saw all the movies. My parents were open till nine at night, I'd sit in the movies until they closed the store. Every Saturday, they'd show cliffhangers.

"The Catholic school would hold a St. Patrick's Day talent

show fundraiser. They let us out of school early. St. Patrick's Day brought out all the talent, and there was a lot of local talent, including the Moylan Sisters. They were on the radio and they put us on the map. They were from Sag Harbor and did perform locally.

"They were our claim to fame.

"I'm 87, I went to the movie theater until the day it burned. A few years ago when I went to the movies, I said they have the same furniture in the ladies room, as forever. I remember that wicker furniture from when it was posh."

GERTRUDE KATZ MEMORIES

COURTESY OF *DAN'S HAMPTONS MEDIA*

Flashlights in the Dark

Harry Fick became manager of the cinema in the late 1940s. For the next 30 years, Fick, who would go on to become Sag Harbor's mayor, was a highly visible presence at the theater and he kept the place running like clockwork. Even today, the Sag Harbor Theatre in the 1950s and 1960s occupies a special place in the hearts of those who grew up here. People can still recite by heart the quirky rules that were meticulously enforced by Fick and his team of ushers and usherettes.

The smoking section was on the left, adults sat in the middle, and unaccompanied minors were banished to the right side of the theater. In their black skirts and white blouses, high school age usherettes showed patrons to their seats with flashlights and did their best to enforce the rules in the dark. This was a particular challenge for employees who were the same age as the teenagers they were attempting to supervise.

If you moved to a section where you didn't belong, laughed a little too hard, or dared put your feet up on the seat in front of you, retribution would arrive quickly in the form of a light beam cutting through the dark to land on your face, along with a stern warning to cut it out. If it was Fick himself who held the flashlight, you'd better straighten up or there'd be trouble for sure.

"TV" Spells Trouble

In the early 1950s, television became the new entertainment medium and movie theaters were up against stiff competition as families across America brought television into their lives and homes. To encourage moviegoers, the Sag Harbor Theatre began hosting amateur nights each Thursday between the first and second shows. Violin players, singers, and other local residents would demonstrate talents, and the performer who received the loudest round of applause from the audience would win.

The theater also sponsored beauty pageants, with Harry Fick crowning the winner "Miss Sag Harbor." In 1955, Prudential Theatres opened the Bridgehampton Drive-in and Fick became the manager of that theater as well.

In the late 1950s, all a kid needed to have a great afternoon at the movies in Sag Harbor was 41 cents—25 cents for admission, 10 cents for a small bag of popcorn, and a nickel for the candy bar machine. Water was free, but it cost a penny for the little white cup with a pointy bottom.

All of this was self-serve—even the popcorn came out of a machine. There were no concession-stand employees in those days.

Despite attempts to bring in customers, on October 9, 1960 the Sag Harbor Theatre announced it would shut down for the fall and winter months. At the time, Fick said there was not enough business to justify keeping it open in the off-season. A short time later, community leaders, elected officials, and members of the Progressive Merchants' Association, held a "summit conference" at the Sag Harbor Municipal Building with executives of Prudential Theatres in an attempt to get them to change their mind. In return, the Prudential executives agreed to consider operating the cinema on weekends, but only if they had the "full hearted support" of the community. One idea floated by the merchants was to sell booklets of theater tickets at special rates to help cover expenses. But the theater did close for a while that winter, and, according to the *Sag Harbor Express*, planned to reopen on Friday, March 29, 1961—Easter weekend—with a screening of *Cimarron*, a western. When it was pointed out that March 29 was Good Friday, in keeping with the wishes of the local village fathers who felt the day should be observed in a more serious manner, Fick agreed to reopen on Saturday, April 1. The following week's offering was *Swiss Family Robinson* and the theater continued to operate Friday through Sunday through the spring. It went back to daily screenings with the arrival of summer.

Miss Sag Harbor winner, Irene DeSanti, with Harry Fick, theater manager. Circa early 1950s.
PHOTO COURTESY OF DEANNA LATTANZIO

"My father, Harry Fick, was mayor of Sag Harbor for six years. He worked for 30 years at the cinema starting in the late 1940s when it was owned by Prudential and the United Artists.

"In the '50s they had talent shows, beauty pageants, and amateur night on Thursday night. It was between the first and second show, around 9 p.m. Some of the local people would get up and play violin or sing. The audience would clap and whoever they clapped for the loudest would win."

CHARLOTTE FAIRLEY MEMORIES

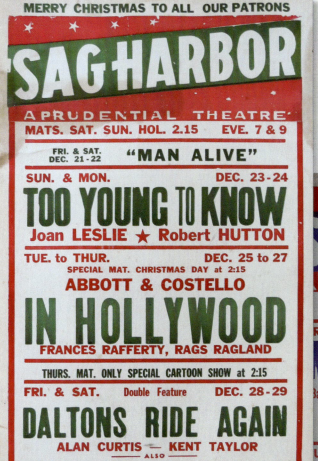

Lobby cards from the 1940s and '50s
COURTESY OF KEVIN MARTIN

WHERE DID THOSE DOTS COME FROM?

In the late 1950s, as televisions began showing up in more and more American homes, movie theaters experienced a decline in attendance. The Sag Harbor Theatre was no exception and in 1961, the cinema's façade was painted with a series of colorful polka dots. Joseph Fiigon, who worked at the theater for many years beginning in 1967, recalled that the dots were the idea of Leonard A. Edwards. Edwards owned the East Hampton movie theater and was the vice president of Prudential Theaters. It was said his inspiration for the paint job was the Wonder Bread wrapper, and though the idea was to attract customers, apparently a lot of people in Sag Harbor did not like the dots at all.

In this photograph, James Fenton noted how shiny the brass fixtures are on the theater's doors. "My grandfather, Harry Fick, was constantly polishing them," he said.

"The polka dots were added in the '60s. We used to sneak out the window onto the roof of the movie theater and drop water balloons over the façade. People thought the polka dots were falling off the building."

BRUCE AND BRAD BEYER MEMORIES

1963 Memorial Day parade
COURTESY OF THE SAG HARBOR EXPRESS

Censoring the Silver Screen

From the time of its debut, the Sag Harbor Theatre was known for running the popular blockbusters of the day with the biggest stars. In October 1961, the film *King of Kings*, about the life of Jesus, played at the theater. In the film, actor Hurd Hatfield, a Sag Harbor resident who attended the screening to talk about the making of the movie, portrayed Pontius Pilate.

But not every film was considered equal, especially by the Catholic Church. Beginning in 1933, the Church sought to assert authority over the film industry by establishing the National Legion of Decency (which in 1965 became the National Catholic Office for Motion Pictures) and implementing a rating system that evaluated films based on their moral acceptability. "A" was morally unobjectionable, "B" stood for morally objectionable in part, and "C" was condemned. The goal of the system was to combat objectionable content in films that the Church felt would have a corrupting effect on youthful innocence. Of course, cynics would say that "C" rated films were more likely to entice young theatergoers than those with "A" ratings.

In any case, around the country church-organized boycotts were regularly held in front of theaters that showed movies with "C" ratings. Sag Harbor was no exception, and in interviews with long-time residents, several recalled how members of the Knights of Columbus would picket in front of the theater in an attempt to dissuade people, particularly fellow Catholics, from entering.

Harry Fick's daughter, Charlotte Fairley, recalled that theater patrons who didn't want to pass the protest line would often go around back where her father would let them in the rear door.

Once the Motion Picture Association of America (MPAA) was established in 1968, movies began being rated with the system that is still used today, and "R" and "X" rated films were added to the list of those that were picketed, if they weren't already on the list.

Mrs. Mortensen
COURTESY OF ANN CHWATSKY

"I was doing the Faces of Sag Harbor portrait series for the Historical Society. I was taking a series of photographs of people who grew up here and still lived here to get the flavor of the village before they were all gone. From going to the movies I had fallen in love with Mrs. Mortensen. I took the photo of her taking the tickets."

ANN CHWATSKY MEMORIES

LOLITA AND HER LOLLIPOP

One movie with a Sag Harbor connection that caused quite a stir was Stanley Kubrick's 1962 film *Lolita*. Based on the controversial novel by Vladimir Nabokov, the film told the story of Humbert Humbert (James Mason) a middle-aged man with an obsession and, ultimately, a sexual relationship with a young girl named Lolita (played by 14-year-old Sue Lyon). The film also starred Shelley Winters as Lolita's overbearing mother and Peter Sellers as the competing middle-aged lover of the adolescent.

The Catholic Legion of Decency wasn't happy about the film. But rather than condemning it outright, the legion bestowed its "Separate Classification" on *Lolita*, and in exchange received an audience age restriction of 18 and over, as well as veto power for all advertising.

That advertising included a poster and newspaper ads featuring Sue Lyon wearing heart-shaped sunglasses and licking a lollipop, with the question "How did they ever make a movie of Lolita?"

Though the film was shot in England, celebrity photographer Bert Stern shot the publicity images of Lyon in Sag Harbor.

The story goes that prior to the film's completion, Kubrick asked Stern to shoot promotional photos of Lyon. Stern chose Sag Harbor as the location and brought the young actress and her mother out for the photo session. But first, Stern stopped

The March of the Multiplexes

On July 9, 1968, United Artists Theatre Circuit Inc. bought all of the cinemas owned by Prudential Theatres. Present at the closing were Joseph Seider, chairman of the board of Prudential Theatres and Salah M. Hassanein, executive vice-president of United Artists Theatres Circuit.

With the sale, the era of the big movie chains had arrived and the blockbusters of the 1970s followed. Movies like *Butch Cassidy and the Sundance Kid* and *Jaws* hit theaters. This was also the era of overly loud "Sensurround" disaster movies—including *Earthquake, Towering Inferno,* and, in the summer of 1977, *Roller Coaster,* which one employee recalled played at the Sag Harbor Theatre on a constant thunderous loop from 10 a.m. to 11 p.m.—even when there was no one in the theater to watch it.

Multiplex theaters became hugely popular by the late 1970s and into the 1980s. In order to maximize profits, large, single screen movie theaters were carved up into several smaller theaters so that many more movies could be shown at once.

United Artists eventually divvied up both the East Hampton and Southampton movie theaters, transforming them into multiplexes. In 1978, the company sold the Sag Harbor Theatre to Gerald Mallow, perhaps because it felt the theater wasn't large enough to subdivide.

When all was said and done, the Sag Harbor Theatre, which had historically had one of the smallest screens on the East End, ended up with the largest.

And under ownership of Gerald Mallow, it also began marching to the beat of its own drummer.

Winter in the Harbor
COURTESY OF ELIZABETH GLASGOW

PART THREE

STANDING THE TEST OF TIME

1978–2016

SAG HARBOR CINEMA 1978-2016

The second life of the Sag Harbor Theatre began in May 1978, when Gerald Mallow bought it from United Artists and renamed it the Sag Harbor Cinema.

Two years earlier, Mallow had purchased the Greenport Theatre on the North Fork. It, too, was a 1930s John Eberson design, and when the Sag Harbor Theatre came up for sale, Mallow, who lives on Shelter Island, liked the idea of owning movie houses on both the North and South Forks.

But Mallow said what really drew him to the Sag Harbor Cinema was the fact that it wasn't a multiplex. With UA out of the picture, Sag Harbor now had the only single-screen theater on the South Fork and the interests of its owner, not corporate marketers, dictated the types of films that would be shown there.

Art House Heaven

The tone was set with *Madame Rosa*—the first film screened at the Sag Harbor Cinema in the summer of 1978. Over the years, it's been said that Mallow bought the theater for his wife, Françoise, who loves European films. When you ask him directly, Mallow doesn't disagree. *Madame Rosa* was a film that Françoise had seen in France and she was eager to see it again. It starred Simone Signoret as an Auschwitz survivor and retired prostitute who cares for the children of other prostitutes.

The concession stand
COURTESY OF GAIL GALLAGHER

This was certainly a stark departure from the mainstream studio fare that had dominated the theater's lineup in previous summers, and Mallow was shocked when nearly 300 people showed up to see *Madame Rosa*.

"I had a positive response from the public. So I kept showing those kind of films," said Mallow. "I was surprised, given what Greenport played. If I tried to show a film like *Madame Rosa* there, it would have had a poor showing."

The theater
COURTESY OF GAIL GALLAGHER

But in Sag Harbor, Mallow found his audience—and they found him. From that point forward, Mallow curated the lineup based on the kinds of films he and Françoise enjoyed—primarily documentaries, unusual foreign flicks, and independent features. Though there were certainly year-round residents among his clientele, a large portion of his devoted audience were weekenders from New York City.

Yes, they shot it here . . .
SWEET LIBERTY, 1986

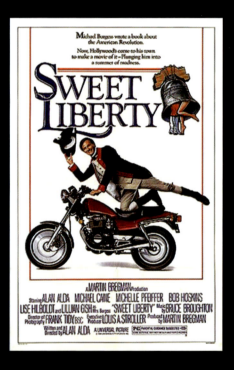

Alan Alda directed, wrote and starred in this comedy, in which he plays a college professor who has written a book about the American Revolution which is being made into a movie. Sag Harbor's Main Street and surrounding areas were the primary locations for the Revolutionary War film within a film setting, and plenty of locals had their time in the limelight. *Sweet Liberty* also starred Michael Caine, Michelle Pfeiffer, Bob Hoskins, and Lillian Gish (in one of her final roles).

COURTESY OF *DAN'S HAMPTONS MEDIA*

This change in the movie-going population reflected what was happening in the wider Sag Harbor community at the time as visitors discovered the village's charm and bought up the old whaling captains' homes and workers' cottages. As those homes were renovated, Sag Harbor became an vital part of their story as well, and for many part-timers, weekends turned into summers, and summers eventually turned into year-round residency.

For fans of the theater, going to the Sag Harbor Cinema, with all its inherent quirks, was an intrinsically endearing part of the small town experience. Even today, lovers of the theater recall wistfully how the radiators clanked, hissed, and banged during the winter months, or the neat fan of napkins thoughtfully provided on the glass candy counter where boxes of Snowcaps, Dots, and Raisinets were ready and able to transport fully grown adults straight back to youth. Many people complained the theater had a musty odor, but for those who loved it, that was an integral part of its charm as well.

While movies took center stage, Mallow also hosted several community-centered events at the theater. Chamber music concerts were a favorite offering, and on several occasions, films were accompanied by lectures or discussions with directors, writers, and actors involved in the production.

THE NIGHT THE STARS CAME OUT

In 2000, Sag Harbor Cinema owner Gerald Mallow teamed up with gallery owner Laura Grenning to offer a star-filled evening of art and film. The event centered around *I Dreamed of Africa*, a film starring Kim Basinger, and the art of painter Marc Dalessio. In the film, which was screened at the Sag Harbor Cinema, Basinger played Kenyan author, environmental activist, and conservationist Kuki Gallmann. At the Grenning Gallery, housed in the retail shop adjacent to the theater entrance, Dalessio exhibited paintings he had recently created while staying on Gallmann's ranch. Both Basinger and her then-husband, Alec Baldwin, were among those who attended the gala one-night screening and art opening, which was one of the biggest events in Sag Harbor that summer and brought a taste of Hollywood glamour to

Laura Grenning with Alec Baldwin in 2000.
PHOTO BY GEIR MAGNUSSON,
COURTESY OF THE GRENNING GALLERY

"The Last Show" by Carl Bretzke, 2017 - oil on canvas
COURTESY / © THE GRENNING GALLERY

Then in 2004, something happened to get the whole community actively involved in the life of the Sag Harbor Cinema.

On the morning of May 10, Brenda Siemer was coming out of her yoga class on Main Street when she saw a work crew removing the iconic Sag Harbor letters from the cinema's façade. Siemer, a documentary filmmaker, artist, and the wife of actor Roy Scheider, felt something was not quite right. On the ground was a replacement sign ready to go up in its place, but Siemer recalled, it bore little resemblance to the original sign.

When she asked the crew where the old sign was going, they told her it was destined for the dump, so Siemer turned to playwright Joe Pintauro who was there on the sidewalk alongside her, and asked what one does in this sort of situation.

"You go to the press," came Pintauro's reply.

That was the moment Brenda Siemer became more than a bystander. She enlisted the help of the staff at the *Sag Harbor Express* to track down a local landscaper with a truck. When the truck arrived at the theater, Siemer and the crew popped the sign into the back of the truck and took it to the Whaling Museum's back lawn for the night. It was then moved to a building on Long Wharf for safekeeping.

Meanwhile, the village's Architectural Review Board, which had not approved the replacement sign, got involved, as did the Sag Harbor police, who paid Siemer a visit at her home to let her know that a report had been filed saying she had stolen the old sign.

Siemer admitted to the crime and quickly made peace with Mallow by spearheading the effort to have an exact replica of the art deco sign made with help from the community.

And that's exactly what happened.

In June 2004, a fundraiser held at a Main Street bistro netted $18,000 for the cause. The following month at Bay Street Theatre's annual benefit,

The original SAG portion of the sign is alive and well and living in Christie Brinkley's house.
COURTESY OF JAKE RAJAS

The new Sag Harbor sign going up.
COURTESY OF CB GRUBB

TOP PHOTO: Gerry Mallow and Brenda Siemer
COURTESY OF CB GRUBB

It was a monumental day!
COURTESY OF CB GRUBB

Christie Brinkley and then-husband Peter Cook paid $30,000 for the "SAG" portion of the old sign during a live auction. Half the money went to the theater; the other half was put toward creation of the new sign. Local fundraising efforts continued in earnest in the months that followed.

Finally, after months of delays and complications (including the disappearance of the initial sign maker who took off with a sizable deposit), the new sign was done and the day was set for its installation on the cinema façade—Saturday, October 20, 2005.

It was late that afternoon, Main Street was blocked off and all of Sag Harbor, it seemed, turned out for the ceremonial lighting of the new sign. In all, Siemer estimates it took close to $50,000 to create those nine iconic neon letters, but they were perfect replicas. It had truly been a community effort, with even the Wharf Shop collecting jars filled with nickels and dimes from people who had bought toys there.

As twilight descended, the switch was flipped and cheers went up from Siemer, Mallow, and the assembled crowd as the new sign was illuminated for the first time. It was at that moment that the entire community truly took ownership of the Sag Harbor Cinema in a way it never had before. The new sign remained a tangible reminder of that commitment and bond, lighting up Main Street every night thereafter . . . until it no longer could.

Sag Harbor Cinema ticket seller Marie Perodin.
COURTESY OF JOHN WICKERSHAM

"What I loved most was the authentic feel of it. It felt like a real old style movie house—the kind from my childhood, like they used to have in East Hampton before they chopped it up and subdivided it. Now you see one wall with sconces and a nice arch and another wall devoid of any character because the theater was chopped down the middle.

"You could experience the entire theater in its integrity, with a wide screen, ample seating, and wonderful art deco style and the lighting.

"I also loved the fact you'd buy the ticket at the window and go down the aisle and buy the popcorn from the same person who sold you the ticket.

"God knows how old the popcorn was. It was very suspicious."

MEMORIES OF EMMA WALTON (AND STEVE HAMILTON)

ALEX KHLUDOV

For several years, Alex Khludov was the maintenance consultant for Gerald Mallow at the Sag Harbor Cinema. At times, his work took him under the lobby floor, up to the roof, and behind walls—which meant he got to know the place as few people did.

"I'll miss the projection booth the most. I thought it was a privilege to go in there," said Khludov. "I liked watching the auditorium through the little window and hearing the ticking of the film.

"There was a very steep wire metal ladder with a shaky handrail—probably the original—to get into the projection booth," he said. "It had a pulley system to get equipment up into it. There was this very complex, very beautiful old-fashioned rotating table which would feed the film into the projector and rewind it back."

Though the projectionist booth was small, Khludov said there was a cavernous room behind the booth where posters from the movies that had played there over the years were rolled up and stored. And as for people who complained that the seats were uncomfortable, Khudlov had this to offer:

"The seats were not original—they were bought from another theater and they were better than the originals. They were a major upgrade from what was there before. People complained about them, but there was nothing to complain about —I know that because the originals were stored there."

Khludov noted that Mallow was unique because he was one of the last independent renters in the business who still showed 35-millimeter films.

"Gerry bought the theater because his wife, Françoise, was a movie buff and he loved her very much," Khludov said. "They'd go all the time. Gerry watched every movie, even if it had already started, he'd pop in for 10 minutes and leave.

"He made every film selection himself, which is why I think this is his legacy," he added. "Everyone appreciated his great job at keeping this almost not for profit theater—not in the legal, but operational sense—going all those years."

Inside the projection booth at the Sag Harbor Cinema.
COURTESY OF MICHAEL HELLER

. . . THE FINAL REEL

On New Year's Eve, 2014, Gerald Mallow hosted a day-long celebration at the Sag Harbor Cinema filled with film, art, and music produced and performed by artists from around the East End. The venture was a collaboration with Sag Harbor singer/songwriter Bryan Downey and the concept was to create a public event that was affordable, fun, and open to all ages.

The festivities began early in the morning with screenings of classic silent films by Buster Keaton, Laurel and Hardy, and Charlie Chaplin—

New Years 2014
COURTESY OF MICHAEL HELLER

films that in all likelihood had been shown nearly 100 years before at one of Sag Harbor's earliest cinemas.

There was also an art exhibition of paintings, sculptures, and photography in the lobby while in the theater itself, actors, poets, and an impressive slate of local musicians performed on stage as people danced in the aisles.

The event was a great example of Mallow's commitment to the cinema and the many ways in which it could be used to serve the community of Sag Harbor.

But by then, times were changing.

New Years 2014
COURTESY OF MICHAEL HELLER

New Years 2014
COURTESY OF MICHAEL HELLER

Back in the summer of 2008, Mallow had quietly placed the Sag Harbor Cinema on the market for $12 million. There were no deals struck and just as quietly, it was taken off the market. But the notion that the beloved cinema might be sold alarmed many in the community who feared it would be transformed into high-end retail space and lost to the village forever.

So in 2009, a group of residents, including artists, screenwriters, and film producers, formed a "Save the Cinema" committee and began formulating a plan to turn the theater into a not-for-profit cinema arts center should the opportunity arise in the form of a long-,term lease or outright purchase. The vision included creating more than one theater so that independent features, documentaries and foreign films could be shown on the large screen, while film series or educational programming could be accommodated in a smaller space.

And that's where things stood until Mallow put the cinema back on the market in early 2016, this time for $14 million. That July, members of the cinema group, under the umbrella of the nonprofit Sag Harbor Partnership, reassembled when Mallow and his wife approached the group to say they wanted to sell the cinema to someone committed to preserving it as a nonprofit theater. Having witnessed the success of the partnership's recent fundraising party on Long Wharf to create a park named for John Steinbeck, Mallow felt that if any group could preserve the theater, this was it.

Over the course of the next several months, the cinema group worked through the details of a purchase of the cinema. It was anticipated that a signed contract would be in place by December 28, 2016.

Then, at around 6:15 a.m. on the morning of Friday, December 16, a Sag Harbor Village police officer noticed a small fire burning near the back of a building adjacent to the theater. It grew quickly, fanned by frigid 20 miles per hour winds from the northwest, and soon it spread out of control. More than 150 volunteers from 19 East End fire departments and ambulance

THE END OF AN ERA, Fire On Main Street 12•16•2016

ALL PHOTOS COURTESY OF MICHAEL HELLER

companies were called in to fight the fire. By the time the flames were extinguished several hours later, four buildings had been gutted or seriously damaged—among them the Sag Harbor Cinema.

Though the auditorium box in back survived, the entire front portion of the theater was entirely destroyed, including the Richard J. Demato Fine Art Gallery, which was housed in the adjacent retail space in the building. The battered, smoke-streaked façade of the cinema remained standing, but by late that evening, it was listing so severely toward the sidewalk that county engineers deemed it too unstable to remain, so it, too, was taken down.

Though the fire left a gaping hole in the center of Main Street, the iconic sign that the community helped create in 2005 was saved after the façade came down. It was put into storage where it awaits the next chapter in the life of the cinema.

Just like those 1930s cliffhangers, nobody can predict exactly what that chapter will entail, but one thing's for certain—Sag Harbor is not the kind of place that gives up easily in the face of adversity.

In an April 2017 interview with the *Sag Harbor Express*, April Gornik, vice president of the Sag Harbor Partnership and a member of the cinema group, said, "Sitting in a theater is like a collective dream. It's such a deep, subconscious experience that bonds you to other people in a really fundamental way."

And what is a movie theater, if not a place for a diverse and vibrant community to come together in the dark and find common ground through a shared experience?

As one Sag Harbor Cinema fan wrote in an online tribute not long after the fire, "I still think of going there for a movie all the time. Fandango still lists it with the caveat 'No movie time listed. Check back.'

"We will all keep checking back."

COURTESY OF LAURA LAMBERT

Artist rendering of the proposed Sag Harbor Cinema Arts Center.
COURTESY OF THE SAG HARBOR PARTNERSHIP

...a word from the SAG HARBOR PARTNERSHIP

The famous sign meant coming home to so many people, even many visiting Sag Harbor for the first time. We drove the long way to go down Main Street before reaching our houses, just to see the sign.

How great it was to have a classic cinema in a harbor village. How fortunate to be in a place of boats and movies and all our rich history. The cinema was a place out of time where, any day, you could watch the best films from the world over. No ads or trailers, just the movies. It took you away to another country, to another life, and you came back knowing more about your own. When the lights came on, you made the long walk up the aisle and down the hallway and emerged onto a perfect Main Street where you felt safe to talk with friends about what you had just experienced. We were travelers in a perfect world.

There aren't many bookstores left anymore, and there aren't many movie theaters, especially like ours. Sitting in a cinema with friends and neighbors and seeing stories on the big screen still has a magic you can't find at home. The Sag Harbor sign is gone for now and Main Street feels so dark, but we are doing everything we can to turn the lights back on. We want to see the red neon glow of our village's name as we stroll down the street. We want it to remind us of where we are. We want to watch those films again to tell us who we are. We are here to help our *Cinema Paradiso* live again.

SELECTED BIBLIOGRAPHY

BOOKS

Bardèche, Maurice, and Brassillach, Robert. *The History of the Movies*. New York: W.W. Norton and the Museum of Modern Art, 1938.

Longmire, Stephen. *Keeping Time in Sag Harbor*. Columbia College Chicago Press, 2007.

Tobier, Nina, ed. *Voices of Sag Harbor: A Village Remembered*. New York: Harbor Electronic Publishing, 2007.

Zaykowski, Dorothy Ingersoll. *Sag Harbor: An American Beauty*. New York: Amereon Limited, 1997

NEWSPAPERS

In addition to the other sources listed on this page, bits and pieces of film lore, history, advertisements, and interesting anecdotes came from various issues of local newspapers, including *The Sag Harbor Corrector*, *The Sag Harbor Express*, *The East Hampton Star* and *Dan's Papers*.

ARCHIVES, PERSONAL DOCUMENTS AND JOURNAL ARTICLES

"Illustrated Songs," *Moving Picture World* 12 December 1908: 472; *Motion Picture Work* by David S. Hulfish, Chicago American School of Correspondence, Chicago, IL: American Technical Society 1913.

MaryEllen LeClerc's scrapbook

Levin, Steve. "A John Eberson Scrapbook." Theatre Historical Society of America, *Annual No. 27-2000*. Pittsburgh, PA: The John and Drew Eberson Architectural Records Archive.

Innovating Silent Cinema: The Papers of Harry & Roy Aitken. Madison. WI: Wisconsin Center for Film and Theater Research Archives.

Williams, Celeste M., and Froehlich, Dietmar. *"John Eberson and the Development of the Movie Theater: Fantasy and Escape."* University of Houston. Helsinki: 91st ACSA International Conference, July, 2003.

Koszarski, Richard. Flu Season: *"Moving Picture World" Reports on Pandemic Influenza, 1918-19" Film History.*

Vol. 17, No. 4, Unfashionable, Overlooked or Under Estimated, pp. 466-485. Bloomington: Indiana University Press, 2005.

INTERNET SOURCES

Other information on film history and technology came from websites including americanstudies at University of Virginia, Artnet, atomsandnumbers, cinematreasures, Criterion, filmsite, Flickr, fromthevaults-boppinbob, IMDb, Nationalgeographic and NYPost.

ACKNOWLEDGMENTS

This book would not have been possible without the enthusiastic support and unending assistance of several people, including April Gornik and Nick Gazzolo of the Sag Harbor Partnership; Jean Held and Dorothy Zaykowski from the Sag Harbor Historical Society; Bryan Boyhan and the staff of the Sag Harbor Express; Sue Mullin and her coworkers at the John Jermain Memorial Library in Sag Harbor.

Also instrumental in providing research, great stories, editorial support and historic visuals were: Melanie Fleishman, Jack Youngs, Joe Markowski, Dell Cullum, Bruce Backlund, Maryellen LeClerc, Deanna Lattanzio, Bruce and Brad Beyer, and Nancy Remkus. Special thanks to Susan Hanley for putting together the team for this book.

Finally, to all the photographers, artists and residents who so generously shared their images and their memories with us, thank you so much. It takes a village.

ANNETTE HINKLE is a writer, journalist and editor on the East End of Long Island. A former associate editor at *The Sag Harbor Express*, she is currently the community news editor of the *Shelter Island Reporter*. Annette has written about the area's cultural scene and has also covered environmental issues and politics.

Over the years, Annette has won multiple New York Press Association awards for her work. She is a long-time regular on the *Media Mavens*, a weekly radio news show hosted by Bonnie Grice in Southampton, N.Y. Annette lives with her family in East Hampton, New York.